MICROSOFT OFFICE 365 FOR BEGINNERS

Practical step-by-step manual,
Microsoft Excel, learning
basic and advanced features
formulas with clear examples.

David R. Malley

Copyright ©2023 David R. Malley

Table Of Contents

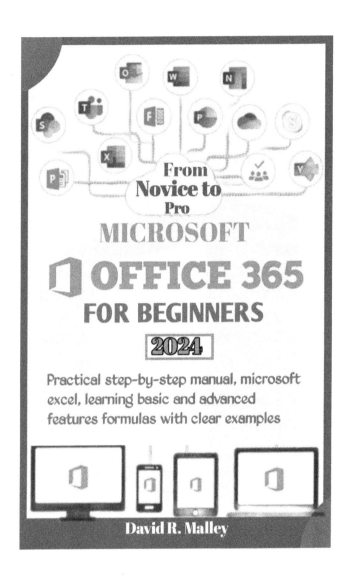

From
Novice to
Pro
MICROSOFT
OFFICE 365
FOR BEGINNERS
2024,

Practical step-by-step manual, microsoft
excel, learning basic and advanced
features formulas with clear examples

David R. Malley

Introduction

Welcome to the world of Microsoft Office 365, a dynamic and versatile suite of productiveness equipment designed to transform the way you work. In this introductory section, we'll delve into the essence of Microsoft Office 365, exploring its core aspects and addressing the necessary question: Why use Microsoft Office 365?

1.1 What is Microsoft Office 365?

Microsoft Office 365 is a cloud-based suite of purposes and services that brings collectively familiar Microsoft Office functions like Word, Excel, PowerPoint, and Outlook, alongside effective collaboration and conversation tools. Unlike traditional standalone Office versions, Office 365 operates on a subscription model, imparting customers a bendy and consistently evolving set of tools and features.

The coronary heart of Office 365 lies in its cloud-based nature. This means that your documents, emails, and collaborative initiatives are no longer restrained to a single device or location. Instead, they are securely stored in the cloud, permitting you to get right of entry to and work on them from honestly anywhere with a web connection. This cloud-centric method fosters seamless collaboration, real-time updates, and a more dynamic workflow.

Office 365 extends past the ordinary desktop applications, incorporating online variations of the Office suite, file storage with OneDrive, verbal exchange equipment like Microsoft Teams, and superior elements for data evaluation and commercial enterprise intelligence. The integration of these elements creates a comprehensive ecosystem, empowering people and businesses to work efficiently, collaboratively, and creatively.

1.2 Why Use Microsoft Office 365?

The choice to embrace Microsoft Office 365 is driven by way of a multitude of compelling reasons:

Flexibility and Accessibility:
Office 365 transcends the barriers of traditional office setups. With cloud-based storage and applications, you can get the right of entry to your work from any device, whether it's a desktop computer, laptop, tablet, or smartphone. This flexibility ensures that your productiveness is now not tethered to a unique location.

Collaboration in Real Time:

Office 365 introduces a new era of collaboration. Multiple customers can work on the same report simultaneously, whether they are in the same room or across distinctive continents. Real-time co-authoring in functions like Word and PowerPoint allows seamless teamwork, fostering creativity and efficiency.

Continuous Updates and Improvements:
By opting for Office 365, you align yourself with a platform that is always evolving. Microsoft constantly releases updates, introducing new features, security enhancements, and performance improvements. This ensures that you continually have access to brand-new equipment and

capabilities, staying in advance in the hastily changing digital landscape.

Integrated Communication Tools:

Office 365 includes conversation equipment like Microsoft Teams, imparting a centralized hub for team collaboration. Whether it is chat, video conferencing, or file sharing, these built-in tools streamline communication, breaking down silos and enhancing teamwork.

Enhanced Security and Compliance:

Security is a pinnacle priority in Office 365. Microsoft employs sturdy safety measures, such as statistics encryption, multi-factor authentication, and superior threat intelligence. Compliance aspects make sure that your agency can meet industry-specific regulatory requirements.

Scalability for Businesses:
Office 365 is scalable, making it suitable for corporations of all sizes. Whether you're a small startup or a giant enterprise, the subscription-based mannequin allows you to scale your usage following your needs. This adaptability ensures cost-effectiveness and efficiency.

In essence, Microsoft Office 365 is not only a suite of applications; it is a transformative method for productivity. Whether you're a personal user, a student, or part of a large organization, Office 365 empowers you to work smarter, collaborate seamlessly, and adapt to the evolving needs of the current workplace. As we embark on this exploration of Office 365, let's uncover the myriad methods it can increase your work journey and redefine what's possible in the realm of productivity tools.

Chapter 1: Getting Started

Welcome to the foundational chapter of your Microsoft Office 365 journey. This chapter will guide you via the integral steps to set up and navigate your Office 365 account, offering you a solid starting factor for a seamless experience.

1.1 Creating a Microsoft Account

Before diving into the intricacies of Office 365, you want a Microsoft account to get entry into its suite of applications and services. If you do not have one, this is a step-by-step guide to creating your Microsoft account:

Steps to Create a Microsoft Account:

Visit the Microsoft Account Creation Page:

Open your desired net browser and go to the Microsoft account advent page.
Click on "Create Account":

Locate the choice to create a new account and click on it.
Fill in the Required Information:

Provide the fundamental information, which includes your email address, password, and non-public details.

Verify Your Identity:

Follow the prompts to affirm your identity, generally through a safety code sent to your email or phone.
Agree to Terms and Conditions:

Read and agree to Microsoft's phrases and conditions.
Complete the Setup:

Finalize the account setup process, and congratulations – you now have a Microsoft account!

1.2 Navigating the Office 365 Dashboard

Now that you have a Microsoft account, let's discover the Office 365 dashboard. The dashboard serves as your central hub for having access to applications, files, and collaboration tools.

Steps to Navigate the Office 365 Dashboard:

Log In to Office 365:

Open your net browser and navigate to the Office 365 login page. Sign in with your newly created Microsoft account credentials.
Explore the App Launcher:

Once logged in, you may locate the App Launcher icon (grid of squares) in the upper left corner. Click on it to divulge a menu of accessible applications.
Access Office Applications:

From the App Launcher, you can get entry to various Office functions like Word, Excel, PowerPoint, and more. Click on the desired app to launch it.
Navigate to OneDrive:

OneDrive is your non-public cloud storage in Office 365. Click on the OneDrive icon to get entry to and manipulate your files saved in the cloud.
Explore Other Services:

Navigate through the dashboard to discover extra offerings such as Outlook for email, Teams for collaboration, and SharePoint for report management.

1.3 Understanding the Office 365 Subscription Plans

Office 365 provides a variety of subscription plans catering to exceptional needs, whether or not you are an individual, a student, or part of an organization. Understanding these plans ensures that you pick out the one that aligns with your requirements.

Common Office 365 Subscription Plans:

Microsoft 365 Personal:

Ideal for personal users, this graph includes access to Office apps on one device, 1TB of OneDrive

storage, and extra points like Outlook, PowerPoint, and Excel.
Microsoft 365 Family:

Designed for families, this graph extends the advantages of Microsoft 365 Personal to a couple of users. Each consumer receives their own set of Office apps and 1TB of OneDrive storage.
Microsoft 365 Business Plans:

Tailored for small to large businesses, these plans offer superior aspects such as business email, Microsoft Teams, and collaboration tools. Plans fluctuate based on organizational size and requirements.
Office 365 Education Plans:

Specifically for college students and educators, these plans furnish access to Office apps, collaborative tools, and cloud storage for educational purposes.

How to Choose the Right Plan:

Identify Your Needs:

Consider your usage requirements, whether it is for private use, household collaboration, or commercial enterprise operations.

Review Features:

Examine the points provided in each plan. Consider whether or not you need superior commercial enterprise equipment or if a personal sketch fits your needs.

Evaluate Storage Needs:

Assess the quantity of OneDrive storage supplied in every plan. This is essential for humans and companies with various facts storage requirements.

Consider Collaboration Tools:

If collaboration is a key component of your work, prioritize plans that encompass Microsoft Teams, SharePoint, and other collaborative features.

By following these steps, you will not solely have a Microsoft account and a draw close of the Office 365 dashboard but additionally a clear appreciation of the subscription plans available. In the subsequent chapters, we will delve deeper into the applications, features, and advanced functionalities that Office 365 has to offer, ensuring you make the most of this powerful suite of tools.

Chapter 2: Exploring Office Applications

Welcome to the core of Microsoft Office 365 – the suite of effective and versatile purposes that redefine the way you create, collaborate, and communicate. In this chapter, we will discover each Office application, presenting insights into their points and realistic usage.

2.1 Word Online: Document Creation and Collaboration

Overview:

Microsoft Word Online brings the energy of phrase processing to your web browser. It lets you create, edit, and collaborate on archives in real time, making it a top-notch device for collaborative writing and file management.

Key Features:

Real-Time Collaboration:
Work on documents concurrently with others, seeing edits in real time.
Cloud Storage Integration:
Save your documents at once to OneDrive, ensuring accessibility from any device.
Formatting Tools:
Access a variety of formatting choices for text, images, and web page layout.

Review and Commenting:
Provide and acquire remarks through feedback and song changes.
Practical Uses:

Create professional files such as reports, resumes, and letters.
Collaborate with team members on venture proposals and documentation.
Review and edit archives seamlessly with colleagues, regardless of location.

2.2 Excel Online: Spreadsheets and Data Analysis

Overview:

Excel Online is your go-to utility for spreadsheet creation, data analysis, and visualization. Whether you are managing finances, examining data sets, or growing charts, Excel Online brings these competencies to your web browser.

Key Features:

Collaborative Spreadsheets:
Work on spreadsheets concurrently with others, facilitating collaborative information analysis.
Formulas and Functions:
Leverage a vast variety of formulations and features for statistics manipulation and calculations.
Chart Creation:

Generate dynamic charts and graphs to visually represent data.

Data Validation:
Ensure factual accuracy with validation policies and error checking.

Practical Uses:

Track and manipulate budgets, expenses, and financial data.

Analyze and visualize statistics sets using charts and graphs.

Collaborate on project timelines and undertaking lists with group members.

2.3 PowerPoint Online: Creating Dynamic Presentations

Overview:

PowerPoint Online empowers you to create engaging and dynamic presentations that captivate your audience. With a host of facets and seamless collaboration, it is your gateway to impactful storytelling.

Key Features:

Real-Time Collaboration:
Collaborate with others on presentations in real time.
Design and Animation:
Access a range of graph tools and animations to decorate your slides.
Slide Show Rehearsal:
Rehearse your presentation and get timing recommendations.
Cloud Storage Integration:
Save and get entry to presentations immediately from OneDrive.
Practical Uses:

Create compelling business presentations with multimedia elements. Collaborate on pitch decks and project proposals with team members. Rehearse and refine displays for impactful delivery.

2.4 OneNote: Organizing Notes and Ideas

Overview:
OneNote is your digital notebook, allowing you to seize and arrange notes, ideas, and information. Whether it's meeting notes, brainstorming sessions, or research, OneNote maintains the whole thing in one place.

Key Features:

Note Organization:
Create notebooks, sections, and pages to arrange your content.
Drawing and Sketching:
Use digital ink to draw and diagram without delay in your notes.
Tagging and Search:
Tag notes for convenient categorization and use powerful search features.
Collaboration:
Collaborate with others in real-time on shared notebooks.
Practical Uses:

Take and arrange meeting notes with ease.

Brainstorm and seize thoughts collaboratively with team members.
Use OneNote as a digital whiteboard for sketches and diagrams.

2.5 Outlook: Email and Calendar Management

Overview:
Outlook is your comprehensive tool for email communication, calendar management, and more. With a center of attention on productivity, Outlook keeps you organized and connected.

Key Features:

Email Management:

Organize and control emails efficiently with folders and filters.

Calendar Integration:

Schedule appointments, meetings, and occasions seamlessly.

Task Management:

Create and control tasks to stay organized.

Contact Management:

Keep a song of contacts and their information.

Practical Uses:

Efficiently manipulate your e-mail inbox with sorting and filtering.

Schedule and organize conferences and appointments with the calendar.

Use duties to create to-do lists and control your workload effectively.

As we explore these Office applications, you'll find out their versatility and collaborative capabilities, setting the stage for more suitable productiveness in your non-public and expert endeavors. Stay tuned as we delve deeper into every application, supplying hands-on guidance to unlock their full potential.

Chapter 3: Collaborative Features

Collaboration lies at the core of Microsoft Office 365, remodeling the way groups work together and fostering a seamless trade of ideas. In this chapter, we will delve into the collaborative aspects that make Office 365 a powerhouse for teamwork, including real-time co-authoring, file sharing, Microsoft Teams, and SharePoint Online.

3.1 Real-time Co-authoring

Features:

Real-time co-authoring is a groundbreaking characteristic that permits a couple of customers to edit a report simultaneously. Whether you're working on a Word document, Excel spreadsheet, or PowerPoint presentation, changes made by one consumer are right away visible to others. This characteristic is no longer restrained to simply online collaboration; it extends to the computing device functions as well, developing a dynamic and synchronized enhancing experience.

Creation:
To provoke real-time co-authoring, begin by opening a document in one of the Office functions online. Share the report with collaborators

with the aid of clicking on the "Share" button, and invite them by way of email. Collaborators can be part of the file by clicking on the shared link.

Uses:
Real-time co-authoring is worthwhile for group projects, team reports, and collaborative content creation. It reduces the want for back-and-forth communication, as group members can work on the document simultaneously, presenting instantaneous comments and edits. This feature enhances productivity and quickens mission timelines.

3.2 Sharing and Collaborating on Documents

Features:
Sharing files in Office 365 goes beyond electronic mail attachments. The platform provides strong sharing options, permitting users to share documents with precise people or make them on hand to an entire team. Access stages can be customized, granting view-only or modifying permissions.

Creation:
To share a document, open the file in the respective Office utility online. Click on the "Share" button, and a dialog field will appear, allowing you to enter the e-mail

addresses of collaborators. You can pick out whether or not they can edit or only view the document.

Uses:
Sharing archives streamlines collaboration by presenting a centralized location for crew members to get admission to and work on files. Whether it is a shared price range spreadsheet, a mission idea in Word, or a collaborative presentation in PowerPoint, this feature ensures that all people are on the same page, promoting transparency and efficiency.

3.3 Using Teams for Communication and Collaboration

Features:
Microsoft Teams is a complete collaboration platform within Office 365 that integrates chat, video conferencing, file sharing, and software integration. It serves as a hub for team communication, fostering a collaborative environment.

Creation:
To create a team, open Microsoft Teams and click on "Join or create a team." Choose whether or not you favor creating a crew from scratch or using a current template. Once the crew is created, you can add

members, and channels, and customize settings.

Uses:
Microsoft Teams is best for digital group collaboration. It brings collective chat, meetings, files, and apps into one workspace, allowing groups to talk seamlessly, share documents, and collaborate on projects. Whether your group is in the same office or scattered globally, Teams gives a centralized platform for tremendous collaboration.

3.4 SharePoint Online: Document Management and Collaboration

Features:

SharePoint Online is an effective record administration and collaboration platform that allows groups to create, share, and manipulate content. It offers a centralized location for storing documents, model control, and seamless collaboration.

Creation:
Creating a SharePoint site involves navigating to the SharePoint touchdown page, deciding on "Create site," and selecting a template primarily based on your team's needs. You can customize the site's structure, permissions, and settings.

Uses:
SharePoint Online serves as a centralized repository for group

documents. It enables collaborative editing, model records tracking, and integration with other Office 365 apps. SharePoint is in particular recommended for large groups or businesses where report administration and collaboration are fundamental elements of daily operations.

As you explore these collaborative features inside Microsoft Office 365, you unlock a new dimension of productiveness and efficiency. Real-time co-authoring, record sharing, Microsoft Teams, and SharePoint Online work harmoniously to create a collaborative ecosystem that empowers groups to work seamlessly, regardless of geographical locations or time zones. These facets redefine the traditional boundaries of teamwork, making collaboration an imperative and streamlined phase of your Office 365 experience.

Chapter 4: Cloud Storage and Security

In the ever-evolving panorama of digital workspaces, the mixture of cloud storage and sturdy protection features is paramount. Microsoft Office 365 excels in offering a seamless combination of cloud storage options and advanced safety measures.

This chapter delves into the essentials of OneDrive for storing and syncing files in the cloud, managing version history, and exploring the protection elements that shield your information inside the Office 365 environment.

4.1 OneDrive: Storing and Syncing Files in the Cloud

Storing Files:
OneDrive, Microsoft's cloud storage solution, provides customers with an impenetrable and accessible area to save files of several types. Whether it is documents, images, or videos, OneDrive presents a centralized repository handy from any machine with a web connection.

Syncing Files:
OneDrive's syncing competencies make sure that your archives are seamlessly up to date across all your devices. As you make changes to a document on your desktop,

these adjustments are instantly reflected on your laptop, tablet, or cellular device. This synchronization ensures that you have the contemporary version of your archives at your fingertips.

Creation:
To shop files in OneDrive, really log in to your Microsoft account, go to OneDrive, and upload documents or create new documents at once within the platform. The intuitive interface lets in handy agency of archives into folders, making it a simple answer for men and women and teams alike.

Uses:
OneDrive is ideal for people and teams who require admission to their archives from multiple

devices. It allows collaboration by way of allowing team individuals to work on an identical document, ensuring all people have the modern version. OneDrive's seamless integration with other Office 365 functions enhances its versatility.

4.2 Managing Version History and Document Recovery

Version History:
Version manipulation is an imperative component of collaborative work, and Office 365 gives robust equipment for managing version history. Every alternative made to a file in OneDrive is tracked, allowing users

to evaluate and fix preceding versions. This function ensures transparency and accountability in collaborative projects.

Document Recovery:
Accidents happen, and files may be accidentally deleted or modified. Office 365's record recuperation characteristic allows customers to repair archives to a preceding state, mitigating the danger of facts loss. The potential to get better documents, even after changes are made, provides peace of mind in the face of unforeseen challenges.

Creation:
Version records are routinely tracked in OneDrive, getting rid of the need for manual intervention. Users can access version history by

choosing a file, clicking on "Version history," and reviewing the listing of versions. Document restoration is a straightforward process, allowing users to fix a record to any point in its version history.

Uses:
Version history and report recovery are in particular treasured in collaborative projects where more than one contributor is working on the same document. This ensures that unintended modifications or deletions can be rectified promptly, preserving the integrity of shared documents.

4.3 Security Features in Office 365

Data Encryption:
Office 365 employs strong information encryption methods to shield your documents each in transit and at rest. This ensures that your information stays confidential and secure, safeguarding it from unauthorized access.

Multi-Factor Authentication:
Enhance the safety of your Office 365 account with multi-factor authentication. This extra layer of protection requires users to verify their identity through a couple of methods, such as a password and a verification code despatched to a mobile device.

Threat Intelligence:

Office 365's risk brain abilities provide proactive protection against cyber threats. The platform utilizes superior analytics to identify and mitigate conceivable safety risks, ensuring secure surroundings for your data.

Creation:
Enabling security aspects in Office 365 entails gaining access to the Security

Chapter 5: Customization and Personalization

One of the strengths of Microsoft Office 365 lies in its adaptability to go well with personal preferences and organizational needs. In this chapter, we will explore a variety of ways users can personalize their Office 365 experience, from tailoring settings to personalizing purposes and enhancing performance through add-ins.

5.1 Customizing Office 365 Settings

User Profile Customization:

Start by personalizing your consumer profile within Office 365. Access the settings menu to replace your profile picture, contact information, and notification preferences. This no longer only provides personal contact but also helps colleagues identify you within collaborative environments.

Language and Regional Settings:
Customize the language and regional settings to shape your preferences. This ensures that the user interface, dates, and numbers are introduced in a format that is convenient and comfy for you.

Theme and Color Scheme:
Tailor the visual aesthetics of your Office 365 environment using selecting a theme and color scheme

that suits your taste. Whether you decide upon a light or dark background, Office 365 permits you to customize your workspace for the finest visible comfort.

Creation:
To customize your Office 365 settings, log in to your account and navigate to the settings menu. Here, you can update your profile details, and language preferences, and pick out a theme/color scheme that resonates with your style.

Uses:
Customizing settings enhances the overall consumer experience, making Office 365 a personalized workspace that aligns with your preferences. Whether you are a male or woman consumer or a

section of a team, these personalized settings contribute to a greater comfortable and environment-friendly working environment.

5.2 Personalizing Your Office Applications

Quick Access Toolbar:
Take advantage of the Quick Access Toolbar in your Office applications. Customize it with the aid of adding regularly used commands, making sure that essential tools are always within convenient reach.

Ribbon Customization:
Tailor the Ribbon in Word, Excel, and other purposes to streamline your workflow. Remove needless

tabs and add frequently used instructions to create a Ribbon that aligns with your precise tasks and preferences.

Template Personalization:
Create and customize templates in Word, Excel, and PowerPoint. Save your custom-made templates for several kinds of documents, spreadsheets, and presentations, allowing for consistency and efficiency in your work.

Creation:
To personalize Office application settings, open the application, go to the "File" or "Options" menu, and explore customization options. Customize the Quick Access Toolbar, Ribbon, and templates following your preferences.

Uses:
Personalizing Office applications optimizes your workflow, making sure that the equipment and commands you use most frequently are easily accessible. This not only saves time but also contributes to a greater intuitive and straightforward experience.

5.3 Adding and Managing Add-ins

Exploring the Office Store:
Discover a wealth of extra functionalities by way of exploring the Office Store for add-ins. Whether it is a tool for assignment management, language translation, or productiveness enhancement,

the Office Store provides a variety of add-ins.

Adding Add-ins:
Integrate add-ins seamlessly into your Office applications. Browse the Office Store, find the add-ins that suit your needs, and add them to your purposes with an easy click.

Managing Add-ins:
Take manipulation of your add-ins by managing them efficiently. Disable or get rid of add-ins that are no longer needed, making sure that your Office surroundings remain clutter-free and tailor-made to your unique requirements.

Creation:
To explore and manage add-ins, open an Office application, go to

the "Insert" or "Insert Add-ins" tab, and get the right type of entry to the Office Store. From here, you can explore, add, and manipulate the add-ins that beautify your productivity.

Uses:

Add-ins lengthen the functionality of Office applications, offering specialized equipment and features. Whether you need to integrate mission management tools, language translation services, or different productiveness enhancers, add-ins permit you to customize your Office ride based on your unique requirements.

As you navigate via the customization and personalization alternatives in Office 365, you empower yourself to tailor your digital workspace following your preferences and workflow. These personal touches not only contribute to an extra exciting and comfortable work environment but also decorate your usual effectiveness and productivity inside the numerous landscapes of Microsoft Office 365.

Chapter 6: Tips and Tricks for Efficiency

In this chapter, we will discover a collection of worthwhile pointers and tricks to supercharge your effectiveness inside Microsoft Office 365. From getting to know keyboard shortcuts to leveraging time-saving aspects and troubleshooting common issues, these insights are designed to elevate your productivity and streamline your workflow.

6.1 Keyboard Shortcuts for Office Applications

Efficient Navigation:
Mastering keyboard shortcuts is a game-changer for environment-friendly navigation within Office applications. Learn common shortcuts such as Ctrl C (Copy), Ctrl V (Paste), and Ctrl S (Save) to streamline your everyday tasks.

Application-Specific Shortcuts:
Each Office software comes with a set of unique shortcuts. For example, in Excel, Ctrl Arrow keys can shortly navigate through data, whilst in Word, Ctrl B (Bold) and

Ctrl I (Italic) decorate text formatting. Familiarize yourself with application-specific shortcuts to expedite your work.

Custom Shortcuts:
Create custom keyboard shortcuts for your frequently used commands. Access the "Customize Ribbon" or "Quick Access Toolbar" options in your Office to assign personalized shortcuts, optimizing your workflow further.

Creation:
To view and customize keyboard shortcuts, navigate to the "File" or "Options" menu in your Office application. Look for the "Customize Ribbon" or "Quick Access Toolbar" section, the place

where you can explore current shortcuts and create custom ones.

Uses:
Keyboard shortcuts drastically minimize the reliance on mouse clicks, accelerating your work pace and enhancing basic efficiency. Incorporate these shortcuts into your day-by-day hobbies to grow to be a more informed Office 365 user.

6.2 Time-Saving Features in Office 365

Tell Me Feature:
Use the "Tell Me" characteristic to quickly locate the instructions you need. Simply kind your question or command into the search bar, and

Office 365 will provide immediate suggestions, supporting you stumble on features besides navigating through menus.

Quick Access Toolbar Customization:
Tailor the Quick Access Toolbar to encompass your most frequently used commands. This toolbar affords one-click access to quintessential features, saving you time by disposing of the need to navigate through a couple of tabs.

Smart Lookup:
Leverage the Smart Lookup feature for quick entry to definitions, Wikipedia entries, and online records associated with the content material in your documents. Highlight a phrase or phrase,

right-click, and pick "Smart Lookup" for immediate insights.

Creation:
To use the "Tell Me" feature, genuinely kind your query or command in the search bar at the top of your Office application. Customize the Quick Access Toolbar by deciding on the preferred commands from the "Customize Ribbon" or "Options" menu. Access Smart Lookup by highlighting a word or phrase, right-clicking, and choosing the "Smart Lookup" option.

Uses:
These time-saving points decorate your efficiency with the aid of presenting rapid get-right of entry to information, commands, and

tools. Incorporate them into your daily workflow to streamline your duties and optimize your use of Office 365.

6.3 Troubleshooting Common Issues

Auto-Recovery Features:
Take gain of the auto-recovery points in Office purposes to safeguard your work. In the tournament of a utility crash or unexpected shutdown, these points routinely recover unsaved changes, stopping information loss.

Clearing Cache and Temporary Files:
If you encounter overall performance issues, consider

clearing the cache and transient files. Accumulated cache can affect application speed. Office applications regularly have choices in the settings or selections menu to clear cache and brief files.

Online Support Resources:

Explore online assist assets furnished by way of Microsoft. The Office 365 aid website, neighborhood forums, and knowledge base offer options for frequent issues. Engage with the community and tap into the collective know-how to troubleshoot and resolve problems.

Creation:

Auto-recovery facets are typically built into Office purposes and can be accessed through the healing preferences in the event of a crash. To clear cache and temporary files, navigate to the settings or selections menu in your Office application. For online support, visit the legit Microsoft Office 365 assist website or neighborhood forums.

Uses:

Troubleshooting common issues is an essential skill for every Office 365 user. By leveraging auto-recovery features, clearing cache, and tapping into online help resources, you can unexpectedly address challenges and hold a clean and uninterrupted workflow.

As you combine these hints and hints into your Office 365 routine, you increase your effectiveness and end up a more adept person on the platform. From navigating applications with keyboard shortcuts to saving time with smart facets and troubleshooting frequent issues, these insights empower you to harness the full achievability of Microsoft Office 365 for a seamless and productive experience.

Chapter 7: Advanced Features

In this chapter, we explore the advanced elements inside Microsoft Office 365 that cater to more specialized needs, empowering users with tools for information visualization, business intelligence, survey creation, quizzes, and assignment management.

7.1 Power BI: Data Visualization and Business Intelligence

Data Visualization:

Power BI is a robust business analytics tool that helps data visualization. Create interactive reports and dashboards that transform raw facts into significant insights. Explore a vast range of visualization options, inclusive of charts, graphs, and maps, to correctly talk complex information.

Data Analysis:
Power BI permits in-depth data evaluation with the aid of connecting to a range of facts and sources. Perform advanced analyses, pick out trends, and find patterns that inform strategic decision-making. Leverage aspects like filters and slicers to engage with information dynamically.

Creation:

To get commenced with Power BI, get the right of entry to the Power BI provider or download the Power BI Desktop application. Connect to your records sources, create datasets, and diagram compelling visualizations using the drag-and-drop interface.

Uses:

Power BI is invaluable for specialists concerned with data analysis, enterprise intelligence, and reporting. Whether you are a data analyst, business strategist, or executive, Power BI enhances your ability to make knowledgeable choices primarily based on data-driven insights.

7.2 Forms: Creating Surveys and Quizzes

Survey Creation:
Forms in Office 365 permit customers to create surveys effortlessly. Design customized varieties with quite several query types, which include multiple-choice, text, and ranking questions. Share surveys with a centered target market and acquire responses in real time.

Quizzes:
Forms extend their competencies to create quizzes for academic or evaluative purposes. Define right answers, set factor values, and automate scoring. Forms even provide immediate feedback to respondents upon quiz completion.

Integration with Excel:

Forms seamlessly integrate with Excel, allowing for environment-friendly records management and analysis. Responses amassed through varieties can be exported to Excel for further processing and visualization.

Creation:

Access Forms through the Office 365 portal, create a new form and start including questions. Customize the form's design, settings, and distribution options. For quizzes, enable the quiz mode and configure scoring settings.

Uses:

Forms are ideal for educators, researchers, and agencies searching to collect feedback, behavior surveys, or administer quizzes. Its simplicity, coupled with Excel integration, makes it a versatile tool for record collection and analysis.

7.3 Planner: Project Management with Office 365

Task Management:
A planner is an undertaking administration device that simplifies project management. Create tasks, assign them to group members, and set due dates. The intuitive visual interface offers a

clear overview of the challenge's progress.

Collaboration:

Facilitate collaboration via developing and assigning tasks within Planner. Team contributors can replace venture statuses, add comments, and connect files, fostering a collaborative environment.

Integration with Teams:

Planner seamlessly integrates with Microsoft Teams, permitting a unified assignment management experience. Access Planner immediately inside Teams, ensuring that challenge administration is seamlessly integrated into the team collaboration platform.

Creation:

Access Planner through the Office 365 portal or immediately within Microsoft Teams. Create a new plan, add tasks, and assign them to team members. Utilize the visible board for music development and manage the task effectively.

Uses:

Planner is an amazing preference for groups looking to streamline assignment management. Whether you're planning an advertising campaign, organizing an event, or coordinating day-by-day tasks, Planner presents an intuitive platform for collaboration and task tracking inside Office 365.

As you delve into these superior aspects within Microsoft Office 365, you equip yourself with effective tools for specialized tasks. Power BI enhances your statistics visualization and enterprise brain capabilities, Forms simplifies survey advent and quiz administration, and Planner streamlines undertaking management, collectively contributing to a more comprehensive and environment-friendly Office 365 experience.

Chapter 8: Mobile and Cross-Device Usage

In this chapter, we explore the flexibility of Microsoft Office 365, highlighting its cellular accessibility and the seamless synchronization of records across various devices. These capabilities empower users to stay productive and connected, regardless of their area or the units they use.

8.1 Accessing Office 365 on Mobile Devices

Mobile Apps Overview:

Microsoft Office 365 presents a suite of mobile functions designed to bring productivity to your fingertips. Explore apps such as Word, Excel, PowerPoint, Outlook, and more, tailor-made for cellular devices. These apps supply an acquainted and uncomplicated interface optimized for smaller screens.

Real-time Collaboration:
Experience real-time collaboration on the go. Whether you are reviewing a document, updating a spreadsheet, or collaborating in an email conversation, Office 365's cell apps allow seamless collaboration with colleagues, making sure that you remain relaxed and productive.

Offline Access:

Ensure productiveness even without an internet connection. Office 365's cellular apps allow you to work offline and sync changes when you reconnect. This offline access feature is especially precious for users who need to remain productive all through travel or in areas with confined connectivity.

Creation:

Download the Office 365 mobile apps from the respective app shops (iOS App Store, Google Play Store). Sign in with your Office 365 account to get admission to your documents, emails, and collaborative tasks on your cellular device.

Uses:

Accessing Office 365 on cell units is best for professionals who need to stay productive on the move. Whether you're responding to emails, reviewing documents, or participating with group members, the cell apps ensure continuity and flexibility in your work.

8.2 Syncing Data Across Devices

OneDrive for Cross-Device Access:

OneDrive, integrated with Office 365, serves as a central hub for syncing your files throughout devices. Any modifications made on one gadget are robotically reflected on others, ensuring that you have the brand new model of your files whether or not you're working on your computer, tablet, or smartphone.

Device Compatibility:

Office 365 is designed to be like-minded with a range of units and operating systems. Whether you use a Windows PC, a Mac, an Android tablet, or an iPad, the seamless synchronization of records ensures a steady and accessible experience.

Collaboration Continuity:

Synced statistics ensure continuity in collaboration. Whether you begin a document on your computing device and edit it on your tablet for the duration of your commute, or evaluate it on your smartphone during a meeting, the synchronization of records ensures that each person is on the same page.

Creation:
Enable OneDrive on your gadgets and make sure that automatic syncing is activated. This ensures that your documents, spreadsheets, and displays are always up to date throughout all your devices. Access Office 365 uses one-of-a-kind gadgets: the usage of the same account credentials.

Uses:
Syncing information across gadgets is useful for users who swap between multiple units throughout the day. It ensures a seamless transition between workstations, laptops, tablets, and smartphones,

permitting non-stop productivity and collaboration.

As you embrace the mobile and cross-device competencies of Microsoft Office 365, you empower yourself with the flexibility to work each time and at any place you need. The cellular apps furnish a transportable and straightforward experience, whilst records synchronization across gadgets ensures that you have admission to your modern work, promoting a linked and efficient workflow.

Chapter 9:
Training and
Support Resources

In this chapter, we are going to explore the wealth of coaching and assistance sources available for Microsoft Office 365 users. From reliable coaching materials to community forums and staying updated with the ultra-modern news, these resources are instrumental in bettering your Office 365 understanding and addressing any challenges you may encounter.

9.1 Microsoft Office 365 Official Training Resources

Microsoft Learning Paths:
Explore Microsoft's official studying paths designed to help customers construct skill ability in Office 365. These paths cover a range of aspects, from primary utilization to advanced functionalities. Engage with interactive modules, videos, and assessments to decorate your abilities systematically.

Office 365 Training Center:
Visit the Office 365 Training Center, a legit aid hub presenting a plethora of tutorials, guides, and rapid beginning resources. Whether you are new to Office 365

or in search of in-depth knowledge about unique applications, this core offers complete training materials.

Certification Programs:
Consider pursuing Microsoft certifications to validate your Office 365 skills. Microsoft affords certifications tailored to extraordinary skill ability levels, together with Microsoft Certified: Modern Desktop Administrator Associate and Microsoft Certified: Security, Compliance, and Identity Fundamentals.

Creation:
Access Microsoft's reputable gaining knowledge of paths and the Office 365 Training Center through the Microsoft website. Enroll in

certification applications through the Microsoft Certification website.

Uses:
Official education sources are perfect for people and companies aiming to deepen their understanding of Office 365. Whether you're an end-user, IT administrator, or aspiring professional, these sources provide structured mastering paths to construct expertise.

9.2 Community Forums and Support Channels

Microsoft Community:
Engage with the Microsoft Community, a platform where users share knowledge, ask

questions and grant solutions. Join discussions, try to find advice, and join with a neighborhood of Office 365 users, administrators, and experts.

TechNet Forums:
Explore the TechNet Forums dedicated to Office 365. These boards offer a space for technical discussions, trouble troubleshooting, and collaboration with IT professionals and administrators. Post questions, share insights, and tap into the collective expertise of the community.

Office 365 Support:
Access professional assist channels supplied via Microsoft. Whether it's submitting an aid ticket, the use of

a digital agent, or exploring the Office 365 guide website, these channels provide direct assistance from Microsoft experts.

Creation:

Visit the Microsoft Community and TechNet Forums online to be part of discussions and seek assistance. Access official aid channels via the Office 365 aid website.

Uses:

Community forums and support channels are priceless for troubleshooting issues, seeking advice, and connecting with a broader neighborhood of Office 365 users. Engaging with these systems fosters collaboration and provides options for challenges.

9.3 Keeping Up with Office 365 Updates and News

Office 365 Blog:
Stay informed about the modern-day features, updates, and bulletins through in many instances checking the Office 365 Blog. This legit blog is a reliable supply of news about new functionalities, improvements, and nice practices.

Message Center:
Explore the Message Center inside the Office 365 Admin Center. This function provides administrators with important notifications and updates involving adjustments to the service, making sure that you

stay informed about upcoming modifications.

Subscription to Newsletters:

Subscribe to newsletters or notifications from Microsoft to acquire updates directly in your inbox. Tailor your preferences to ensure you receive records applicable to your utilization and hobbies inside Office 365.

Creation:

Access the Office 365 Blog through the reputable Microsoft website. Navigate to the Message Center inside the Office 365 Admin Center for administrator-specific updates. Subscribe to newsletters through the Microsoft verbal exchange preferences.

Uses:

Staying informed about Office 365 updates and information is quintessential for leveraging new features, optimizing workflows, and maintaining security. Regularly checking the blog, and Message Center, and subscribing to newsletters ensures that you are up-to-date with the latest developments.

By tapping into these education and guide resources, you equip yourself with the expertise and help to navigate the complexities of Microsoft Office 365. Whether you're a novice in search of foundational education or an experienced person searching to continue to be modern with updates, these assets serve as

treasured companions in your
Office 365 journey.

Conclusion

Congratulations on finishing the ride through the complete information on Microsoft Office 365 for beginners. This ride has provided you with a stable basis for understanding, navigating, and harnessing the electricity of Office 365. Let's recap key standards and talk about the subsequent steps in your Office 365 journey.

10.1 Recap of Key Concepts

Introduction to Office 365:

Explored the fundamentals of Microsoft Office 365 and its

position in current digital workspaces.

Getting Started:

Created a Microsoft account, navigated the Office 365 dashboard, and understood subscription plans.

Exploring Office Applications:

Dived into Word Online, Excel Online, PowerPoint Online, OneNote, and Outlook, discovering their elements and uses.

Collaborative Features:

Explored real-time co-authoring, report sharing, Microsoft Teams, and SharePoint Online for high-quality collaboration.

Cloud Storage and Security:

Utilized OneDrive for cloud storage, managed model history, and delved into security elements within Office 365.
Customization and Personalization:

Customized Office 365 settings, customized applications, and explored the world of add-ins for enhanced functionality.
Tips and Tricks for Efficiency:

Mastered keyboard shortcuts, explored time-saving features, and discovered troubleshooting strategies for frequent issues.
Advanced Features:

Leveraged Power BI for statistics visualization, Forms for surveys and quizzes, and Planner for venture management.

Mobile and Cross-Device Usage:

Accessed Office 365 on cell devices, and synced statistics seamlessly throughout devices, ensuring flexibility and continuity.
Training and Support Resources:

Discovered Microsoft's professional training materials, engaged in community forums, and stayed updated via more than a few support channels.

10.2 Next Steps in Your Office 365 Journey

Now that you have a robust basis in Office 365, reflect on consideration on the following steps to continue and deepen your journey:

Advanced Training:

Explore superior training sources to enhance your abilities further. Consider pursuing Microsoft certifications to validate your expertise.

Community Engagement:

Continue participating in neighborhood forums, enticing fellow users, and contributing to discussions. Share your experiences and analyze them with others.

Stay Informed:

Regularly check the Office 365 Blog, and Message Center, and subscribe to newsletters to continue to be knowledgeable about updates, new features, and fine practices.

Apply Knowledge:

Apply your newfound knowledge in real-world scenarios. Implement Office 365 points and functionalities in your daily duties and projects.

Feedback and Improvement:

Provide remarks to Microsoft via reliable channels. Your center contributes to the enhancement of Office 365, making sure that it continues to meet consumer needs.

Remember, Office 365 is a dynamic platform that evolves with technological know-how and personal feedback. By staying engaged, continually learning, and making use of your knowledge, you will not only enhance your private talent but also make contributions to the bright Office 365 community.

Thank you for joining us on this Office 365 journey. Best needs for your continued success in exploring and maximizing the viability of Microsoft Office 365!

www.ingramcontent.com/pod-product-compliance
Lightning Source LLC
LaVergne TN
LVHW022126060326
832903LV00063B/4122